The Taiping Vision of a Christian China 1836–1864

by
Jonathan D. Spence

THE EIGHTEENTH
Charles Edmondson Historical Lectures

Baylor University, Waco, Texas
April 11–12, 1996

MARKHAM PRESS FUND
WACO, TEXAS

This volume is the thirty-third volume published by the Markham Press Fund of Baylor University Press, established in memory of Dr. L. N. and Princess Finch Markham of Longview, Texas, by their daughters, Mrs. R. Matt Dawson of Waco, Texas, and Mrs. B. Reid Clanton of Longview, Texas.

The Charles Edmondson Historical Lecture Series, Number 18.

David W. Hendon, general editor.

Publication of this series of lectures is made possible by a special grant from Dr. E. Bud Edmondson of Longview, Texas.

First edition 1998.

Library of Congress Catalog Card Number: 98-65308
International Standard Book Number: 0-918954-66-5

Printed in the United States of America.

FOREWORD

In 1975 Dr. E. Bud Edmondson of Longview, Texas, began an endowment fund at Baylor University to honor his father, Mr. Charles S. B. Edmondson. Dr. Edmondson's intent was to have the proceeds from the fund used to bring to the University outstanding historians who could synthesize, interpret, and communicate history in such a way as to make the past relevant to the present generation.

Baylor University and the Waco community are grateful to Dr. Edmondson for his generosity in establishing the CHARLES EDMONDSON HISTORICAL LECTURES.

Professor Spence, the eighteenth Edmondson Lecturer, discusses his research into the Taiping Rebellion in 18th-century China, with special emphasis on the religious aspects of the event. In addition to the topic covered, readers are treated to several discussions of how historical research can be carried out.

This edition was created from a transcript of the actual lectures; thus, it should be read with the "sound" of the words in mind rather than as a polished research paper.

****

The views expressed in these lectures are those of the author and do not necessarily reflect the position of Baylor University or of the Markham Press Fund.

****

Although the Charles Edmondson Historical Lectures have been presented annually at Baylor University since 1978, they have not always been available for publication by the Markham Press Fund. A list of previous lectures appears at the end of this work.

LECTURE I

PLANNING AN EARTHLY PARADISE

I sometimes feel it necessary to mention that I came as a graduate student a long time ago to this country, which I'd never visited, and I switched to Chinese studies in graduate school, in Yale. And I simply got so absorbed and fascinated with the subject that I devoted the rest of my life to it. But I want to tell you also that I still consider myself a kind of amateur, and one can interpret an amateur as somebody who continues to love what they're doing as opposed to the professional who gets completely caught up in the day-to-day running of an individual task. In that sense of amateur, I still feel that sense of amazement and excitement at the complexity of Chinese culture and its richness, its subtlety. And we now have the extraordinary developments in China today, and the fact that we have to think about it seriously in economic and political terms, and have to re-think the changing nature of Communism in China itself.

These lecture are in two parts, dealing with what I call "founding a Christian community in China." They deal with an amazing event in the nineteenth century, known by the general description of Taiping Rebellion, which literally means "great peace" or "heavenly peace." For today's lecture I'm going to talk about what I call "planning an earthly paradise." How do you go about planning an earthly paradise in China? There really was a major attempt in the nineteenth century to set up a kingdom of heaven on earth. Many other cultures have tried this; they're still trying it in our own time; they've tried it for millennia of human history.

So let's talk today about the planning and the background. I see the planning for this enormous movement as being what I would call a question of contexts. I want to explore that idea with you today, and then I want to look more at the nature and character of the leader of this movement tomorrow. So today will be a broader historical background and reflection on the history of nineteenth-century China, with the Taiping Rebellion as its focus. Tomorrow we'll get into some more specific country.

The Taiping Rebellion was first of all an astonishing political and religious upheaval. But it intersected with an attempted social revolution, a social revolution that was planned to include the nature of land holding, land ownership, and work on the land, the way that human beings worked at their occupations, and the whole nature of family structure and family organization. It was, in other words, a revolutionary attempt at change.

It was led by a man called Hong, whose name later was changed to Hong Xiuquan, about whom we know quite a bit. However strange this story may seem, this is a historical person who can be studied through a large range of sources both in the public domain and in archival documents. We know that Hong was born in 1814, we know that he was born to a farming family in southeast China, and that he was chosen by his family to work at the examination system of China rather than having to work all the time on the farm. So, in other words, he was freed from the day-to-day hard work on the farm so that he could pursue his studies. In being thus freed, his two elder brothers continued to work on the land. And the sibling relationship in China is a very hierarchical one. An elder brother is much older than a younger brother. The relationship is certainly not as strong as father and son, but it's much stronger than anything that Westerners can imagine as a brotherly relationship. So Hong was free to study while the elder brothers continued to work on the land. And he took the competitive examinations for office in China, based on the Confucian classics. He passed the qualifying exam several times, but each time he failed to make the short list in the actual examination. I want to emphasize this because it can suggest to us the dimensions of psychological pressure that this young man must have been under in the 1820s and 1830s.

We also know historically that in 1836 Hong was handed a text in the town in southeast China where he was working. We know this man's name, we know his background, we know the area he grew up in, and we know that in 1836 he was handed a text. Part of my talk both today and tomorrow is going to be about that extraordinary moment in which one person hands another a text. I'm sure any of you in big cities have been handed a text: people push things in your hands as you cross the street, and you look at the way they're dressed and maybe look at their race or their gender, and maybe you shuffle by or maybe you stop and make eye contact. It's a kind of a moment, a split second, there's not much time to think it through. You take it and throw it away or you feel nervous; maybe you take it and look at it and put it in your pocket. Something like that is what happened here. Hong was handed a text. He took it. He does not seem to have been very careful about reading it, but he didn't throw it away. And all those things had to happen at once to make the story possible. The text was not just a handout, it was not just an advertisement; it was a summary of Christian doctrine with long sections of the Bible translated into Chinese, with Chinese commentary on those sections, and the autobiography of the life of a young Chinese man, again written in Chinese, who had abandoned Buddhism to become a Christian. So if this text could be understood, it was in its center a potentially revolutionary document, a very strange document, and it was the kind of document that had not circulated before this time. Again, we've got to understand the context of how such a thing could happen—not only how the text could be handed over and grasped, but how the text could have the content that it in fact had. And that's a historian's task, trying to work out how such things come about.

We also know that in 1837 this young man, by then twenty-three years old, had a series of visions, and in those visions he embarked on a journey. Again, this is ago-old in terms of human drama, human mental exploration, shamanic journeys or trips to another sphere. We might call them visions, psychic experiences, dreams, good dreams, bad dreams. This was a protracted dream that came after yet another examination failure. And in this dream, Hong traveled to another realm where he met a number of people, including an older man with a beard, a younger man who called him brother, and an older woman, who somehow purified him, washed him clean, and presented him to the older man who seemed to have some kind of paternal relationship to him. In the dreams, also, he was urged by the older man to fight demons. He wasn't told what that meant, but he was urged to fight demons. His family, hovering nervously around his room in southeast China, witnessed the outer manifestations of this dream state. We can say Hong was on the edge of what we might call a coma or some kind of transportation, possession. At this time, he actually acted out the fight against demons. He shouted that he had been called to kill demons, and waved his hands in a sword-like motion. He jumped out of bed, apparently while sound asleep, and with an imaginary sword lashed through the air.

Hong woke up and neither forgot nor understood the dream. Here we could explore the question of whether different cultures interpret dreams the same way. Many of us might have a dream—we wake up and say, "Oh, I've had a dream and it's all about this." In 1830s China, you had a dream and you said, "I had a dream and it deals with this, but I do not have the key, I do not understand it, therefore the dream has no meaning. It's not up to me to create a meaning. I do not have the key." There's no accessibility. So these images stayed in Hong's mind. They were not forgotten, but they could not be explained.

Then in 1843 they were explained. A friend read the text that Hong had not thrown away. If at any time he'd thrown it away, or if his very able and affectionate wife had thrown it away in purging his library, or if he'd moved to a new house, perhaps, we wouldn't have this story either. The text was still on the shelf; a friend borrowed it, read it, and came back to Hong and said, "You ought to read this text you've had lying around here. It's extraordinary." And so Hong read it, and it plunged him into a world in which he read part of the book of Exodus, the opening of Genesis, and several middle chapters of Genesis. He read the whole of the first chapter of the book of the prophet Isaiah, he read most of the Gospel of St. Matthew, and he read the last chapter of the Revelation of John the Divine. That's just a partial selection, but that was the body of the text. And along with these texts went some commentaries, but no real explanation of what those moments from the Bible could mean. There was no explanation of what these extraordinary names were. What was Isaiah? What was Jeremiah? What was Ezekiel? What were these names that came from nowhere using Chinese characters with a sound? And what was a strange figure apparently with enormous power called Yeh-huo-hua? Only later could Hong know that Yeh-huo-hua was, of course, Jehovah, as literally transcribed by the Chinese trying to render the Bible in Chinese form.

There were many other gods in this version of the Bible, not just this Jehovah who had this terrible power. There was a "Lord on High" who was a supreme lord. There were many other phrases used. So Hong had what I think initially he could have interpreted as a multi-divine text. There was no clear sense that this was a monotheistic text because there were different gods' names in it, or names of God, and many strange events. I'll come back to the way he tried to interpret those events tomorrow. But if you know the Bible at all, those, just those, references will show you something of what was going on.

This reading of the Bible, particularly St. Matthew's Gospel, but also some of the other parts, gave Hong the key to his dream. And this was the changing moment in his life. The dream was now understandable by relating those not-forgotten moments of his journey to the newly read but inscrutable text. In particular, Hong understood that the older man in the dream must be God the Father. And the person who called him brother must be Jesus. But since that person had called him brother and seemed to have a special power, and the Bible talked about this man, or this God-man, in an extraordinary way, Hong therefore must be Jesus's younger brother. I want to again emphasize younger, so though we might find this abhorrent or blasphemous, it's still very much a younger brother of Jesus. God was therefore the father in an immediate and personal way. And that is why

I called my own book God's Chinese Son. That was how he saw himself for the rest of his life.

Now, this, again, could have gone nowhere, it could have remained a personal hodgepodge of insights and a mixture of readings of the Bible and interpretation. It might have gone nowhere except that the knowledge that somehow he was in this special family relationship through Jesus to God clearly made Hong a different person—someone stronger, perhaps, more self-confident. Probably not more intelligent or more learned, but he seems to have become somebody who now could attract followers. At first, the number of followers was very small—two. He attracted two followers who thought that perhaps this relationship was an important one and that Hong had somehow taken on a new kind of aura or power. Over the next few years, in a very small village north of what was then Canton City (as the British called it) or Guangzhou, in a little village in the hills, Hong continued to read the texts, continued to think about them, continued to try and think about his role, and from the two, moved to about ten people who began to pray together. Remember that in Matthew's Gospel you have the Sermon on the Mount, and you have the Lord's Prayer, and you begin to get an insight into how to pray and to think together. Though he didn't yet build a church, they apparently met for what we would, I think, call simple Bible reading or prayer sessions. And then very slowly they formed a society called the God Worshipping Society. In 1844, Hong moved to a different area of China, one about 150 miles away, where he had relatives in a very poor part of the hill country. And that move was, again, central to the story.

In this area of China, called Guangxi Province, west of Guangdong Province, among people who were in many cases from a minority group of Chinese called the Hakka, the God Worshippers slowly increased in their numbers, first into the hundreds and then to the low thousands, and by about 1847-48, probably up to about twenty to thirty thousand, and maybe as high as fifty thousand by the end of the 1840s. The accumulation of such a large group who would often pray together and chant together began to attract the attention of the state.

And the moment in which the state decides it is important, first of all, to track such a group, and then perhaps to intervene, was as crucial and sensitive in China as it has proved in other societies. The state didn't really want to intervene; it just wanted to keep law and order, and it tried to decide how the watch should be kept and what was going too far.

The God Worshippers could probably have survived if they had not gone too far. But one of the things we know they did was that in their joy and excitement, if those are the two right words, their sense of destiny, they began to smash temples in the area. They began to destroy idols. So that charge to exterminate demons began to get a more practical sense in Hong's mind and those of his followers. They began to literally trash neighboring temples. That meant they knocked over the idols. They didn't just knock them over, so that the peasants could come back and put them up again—they broke off their heads, they snapped off their arms, they wrote graffiti on the walls with their calligraphic brushes. They took ink with them and smeared the walls with religious messages. They were a new religion, one that made no sense in the communities around the God Worshipping base. So a series of clashes ensued, which led ultimately to a sequence that we can trace: something like local bewilderment, local irritation, local anger, local rage, fisticuffs, shoving about, harassment, until at last somebody got killed. Then local villagers got together and killed someone else. Then some local Qing troops, the Manchu Dynasty's troops, came, and some of them got killed. Now you had an armed conflict. The God Worshippers became the Taiping Heavenly Army. They slowly began to arm in self-defense. They also began to make arms, and they began to store arms, all of which were totally illegal. The Qing state was one that did not want an armed populace at any level under its regime. The laws on that were very strict. Finally, the Taiping became too large, too menacing, they were causing too much trouble to be left alone. So the Qing state moved into active confrontation with regular army troops. Troops had to be deployed, logistics had to be worked out. The officers grew in seniority, from captains to major to colonels. All this can be traced through the Chinese documents. Finally, some pitched battles were launched, the second of which, astonishingly, the Taiping won. It was a very difficult battle. It was a straightforward confrontation with regular troops of the state.

The Taiping won, but the trouble was that their victory just brought greater government reprisals. In a series of very hard-hitting campaigns between 1851 and 1853, they were driven out of their Guangxi base and had to flee. What they decided to do was find the promised land. Hong didn't know where it was. It's one of the things I track in my book,[1] trying to work out when he decided that he knew where the promised land was. On that march away from the enemies who were represented by the state, the Taiping army cut north up to the Yangzi River, very difficult country to fight over. They did this with great tenacity, adding many recruits as they went, with a mixture of messages—partly religious, partly political, partly anti-dynastic, partly simply anti-demon in the very broad sense. In 1853, they seized the huge city of Wuchang on the Yangzi River (where later the 1911 Revolution also broke out), a very strategic, rich city. They captured this against all the odds. It was the first gigantic walled city they'd ever captured. That gave them what big cities used to give you: treasury, stores of arms, huge stockpiles of grain, silver in mounds beyond the dreams of anyone, silks. And with that victory behind them they went down to the city of Nanjing, near the mouth of the Yangzi River, just inland from Shanghai. There, in 1853, they established their kingdom, their Taiping Heavenly Kingdom of great peace, which lasted with Hong as its king until 1864.

Now, what is all this about, and how is it possible? Let's for the rest of today try and think about how this is possible and then tomorrow go back into the details. Let me be up front about something right away. I think that the Taiping is an example of a special kind of history, one that is not the same as some other kinds of history. We can all intersect the discipline of history in many different ways, obviously. We can make our cut in all sorts of places. But perhaps the biggest central separation of the two types of history is this. One is the type of history in which we say, well, these things were bound to happen. This was going to happen anyway. It doesn't really matter who the leaders were, who the individuals were. Then we can narrow this down and say we're dealing with modes of production or ownership of means of production, or we're dealing with massive economic dislocation, or we're dealing with colossal confrontations of races, or whatever it might be. Or we can say, this is a kind of history in which the only way to make certain things possible is for an extraordinary number of things to flow together from many, many different places and points of view, to then coalesce around one individual with a unique mix in his or her own psyche, and thus form their own strange blending. One of my arguments is that the Taiping is very much in this latter category. I don't think this rebellion could have unfolded in the way it did without all the things I'm now going to talk about, plus Hong at the center. We know most of the other people who worked with him, and it doesn't seem to me that they fit the bill for this particular combination. (They might have won when he lost. That's a different question we can reflect on tomorrow.)

So let's try and think of it. If you're planning an earthly paradise in the 1840s and 1850s, what has to flow together? I've put things in sort of a general order. Let's run through them in fairly broad categories and then we can come back to any of them that you wish. This is not an order of priorities, because I find that very hard to work out, but they're all important.

Social Vision

One crosshead would be social vision. That must be somewhere in this mix, to make this possible. What was the context that made this possible for Hong? Well, economic historians come into the picture here as they try to analyze the reality of life in southeast China in the 1830s and 1840s. It was a time in which rural poverty was growing, and, in fact, there was an immiseration, a growing lack of resources in certain areas of southeast China, particularly below Canton and stretching down to the coast. (This is the area, by the way, from which the immense percentage of China's immigrants to this country were to come in the years between 1860 and 1920.) So this was an area that was already feeling extraordinary economic and population pressures, which later were to lead to a major move for the Chinese people into another culture and society.

This poverty and immiseration led to all sorts of problems with land holding, finding and keeping jobs, and finding adequate labor for your family. There was a spread of mining in the area, there was a spread of strip cropping, moving up into hillsides. Of course, when impoverished farmers strip crop the upper levels of hills, they might do fine for a year or two, but then they cause erosion and the desiccation of the uplands and that leads to siltation of the rivers below, because the eroded soil has got to go somewhere, and siltation follows erosion and leads to flooding and related problems. So this was an area in what now we might call ecological trouble mixed with economic trouble.

And this idea, I think, will fit with what we'll see in my next lecture regarding the exact way that Hong tried to structure his social vision. It was to include, as I mentioned in my introductory remarks, the nature of occupations, how we should work, the nature of people and the land they till, and the nature of family structures that could survive in such an environment. And the vision that Hong drew out of this was something very close to what we would now term socialism or com-munitarianism. The social vision slowly brought Hong to reflect on the fact that it would be a better world if people worked the land in common, drew from the fruits of their labor enough for themselves and their families—the families could be as big as they liked, but the families should draw first from the labor. But everything else, everything you didn't need, as that could be defined by the heavenly king or his staff, should be put into a common treasury. Again, there are all sorts of jobs that people have to do, and Hong later was to name carpenters, masons, potters, people with a craft or a building skill. Those skills were needed, but as much as possible everybody should pool together to do such tasks. There should be a blurring of the work patterns. Some of you might think you recognize very early Marxist theory, but there is no interconnection at all as far as anyone has been able to discover from these Chinese tracts. Marxist texts were not circulating in China, nor was Marx yet reading about the Taiping. (Though, by the way, Marx did later read about the Taiping, and write about it.)

The social vision is also mixed with a problem that comes into it and mustn't be neglected. (Again, there's been some excellent historical work on it.) It's what we might call the partial criminalization of the society, the spread of crime, and the spread of dissonant units, particularly in southeast China. Historians of China and indeed the Chinese themselves often give to these the rough label of "secret societies." (And that is what the headlines of our newspapers still do call them, now that secret societies have been proven still strong both in China and in this country.) These secret societies included the Heaven and Earth Society, or Tian Di Hui, and various other groups that were formed in the late eighteenth century for various complex social historical and economic reasons, and were spreading increasingly in this part of China. So we've got poverty and immiseration of the land, tensions, the beginning of a communitarian vision, and the spreading of secret societies and criminal organization.

Law and Order

A second sort of crosshead would be the linking of law and order with Puritanism, or puritan beliefs. Law and order sprang from the desire to hold on to a structure of values in a society that was going through the problems just mentioned. And it was made more difficult by the fact that pirate suppression was occurring at the same time off the China coast; adding a sub-category to this idea of law and order. Pirate suppression was being carried out by the British, and in this strange way this story is linked to Hong Kong, which is so much in our consciousness right now, because next year Hong Kong will return to China. The British seized Hong Kong in 1840. Being law-and-order people, at least in their colonial dependencies, they immediately tried to get rid of the pirates around the island of Hong Kong. They did not kill them all, but they drove them inland. China has rivers stretching from the sea in the east, near Canton, deep into the heart of China toward the west. And it has another group of rivers running north from the South China Sea, cutting into southern China. These river systems converge on Guangxi, the area where the God Worshippers were assembling and growing in numbers. British law and order in Hong Kong, in other words, led to a wash—a literal backwash of criminal elements who had been sea pirates made the transposition into being river pirates. They took over small towns and villages along the banks of the rivers and established a whole network of thuggery and protection rackets in the midst of the farmers in the area, and then linked that with the secret societies. All these things are flowing together in our category number two.

The British did not just bring law and order. They brought opium. And they began to develop the sale of opium in large volume. The beginning of mass sales of opium in China dates from the 1820s. Sales exacerbated in 1834, when Hong was twenty, with the destruction in London of the monopoly of the British East India Company that had existed from the 1600s. This global geopolitical economic shift led to opium flowing into the villages all around where Hong was living as a young man, because the ending of the East India Company threw the China trade open.

Hong was driven into what we might call a broad puritan stance by the presence of the opium and also by the amount of drinking. Hong, for the rest of his life, was passionately against alcohol and against opium. This was savagely enforced among his followers, the God Worshippers; the penalty for drinking or opium smoking was execution. So it was a straightforward disciplinary measure in his eyes to keep order in the ranks and order in the God-fearing community, and also to try and keep the lid on some of the other social programs that he witnessed.

Nationalism

The third of these crossheads is what I would call nationalism, or perhaps the emergence of an awareness of different nations competing in a similar area. In south China, people like Hong saw themselves as both Han Chinese and as Hakka, or minority Chinese. The people who ran the country were Manchus, the Qing dynasty rulers. The Manchus had conquered China in 1644 and they had been the dominant rulers of China all that time, but until the 1830s they had never been humiliated in war by a foreign power. In 1839 and 1840, the British went to war with the Qing state to demand a huge range of new trade concessions, including wider opium distribution, wider missionary endeavor, and wider diplomatic contact. In doing this they began literally to blow the Manchus out of the water. The British brought firepower developed during the Napoleonic Wars, which had ended in 1815. They were free now to concentrate in the Far East. They were free from these huge European wars, the great treaty system that was to last almost a century was falling into place in Europe, and the Industrial Revolution was running full speed. As industrial revolutions tend to do, this included arms manufacture, sophistication in armaments, better exploding shells, better trajectories, better artillery, a move toward better rifling in guns, and so on. It was the Manchus who were defeated. There have been some wonderful studies showing us how, in fact, Manchu-Chinese tensions began to emerge at this time, but that they now got muddled up with the new coming of this outside force (the British) thus contributing to the mix.

What is strange here is that you might assume that this should have made Hong anti-British and pro-Manchu. But it didn't. He seems to have, on the contrary, somehow associated the British more with the providence of the Bible, because the British were among those who brought the Bible to him at this time. Also, those demons from the dream who could not be interpreted slowly began to fix in Hong's mind with the Manchus. This demonology of the conquering race is something one sees in other cultures and civilizations; indeed, the dehumanization of those we intend to discriminate against or kill is a regrettable but perpetual human mode of thought. So the nationalism and the identification of demons leaves the British more or less on the side of the angels—at least, neutral—and the Manchus as demons.

Localism

The fourth of these broad areas, our next crosshead, would be what I call localism; and the local history element is linked, perhaps surprisingly, to a certain amount of freedom for women. Let me explain why.

Hong was a Hakka (to Chinese speakers it's "kejia," or guest people), and the Hakkas were particularly strong in the hill country of Guangxi to which he moved. Hong recruited most easily among Hakkas and he found many of his good leaders among the Hakkas. He also found many of his financial backers among the Hakka because there were wealthy Hakka just as there were struggling Hakka in the hills. There was a loyalty here, a kind of bonding. Other Chinese could enter into this mix, but the Hakkas were strong at the center. The Chinese of this time practiced the social habit of footbinding: the feet of the women, for aesthetic and maybe erotic reasons, were compressed into tiny, very painful condensations of the shape of the foot and this involved breaking the toes. The Hakka, however, had never bound their feet. They didn't think this was correct. Their women worked on the farm, and a bound-foot woman cannot do heavy labor on the farm, nor can she walk far; it's just too painful. Hakka women strode free. And when Hong combined his localist organization with a largely Hakka background, he was willing, and able, to organize the Hakka women—strong, able-bodied women—into military units. But he insisted the women's units and men's units were kept apart. If you crossed from one to the other, you were executed. Until the Taiping got to the promised land, he chose to leave it like that. Each group would fight better. In some recently discovered texts we have found some discussions of Taiping women's units actually going into action. So that is all part of our story.

Confucian Education

Another one of these crossheads would be the traditional Confucian educational system. The Confucian texts had been formalized and adapted and commented on, and had gone through many, many changes, but they still were the basic center of the examination system. They were also the basic center of conventional morality, decent behavior, and family structure in early nineteenth-century China. But Hong had failed in the Confucian examinations, and though he was, I think we can say, a deeply moral person according to his own lights, he nevertheless felt that an alternative morality to the Confucian one could be found which would still hold on to some of the central values. But Confucius, himself, was thrown out, and part of Hong's dream was reinterpreted to show that Confucius had in fact come to heaven, and while there had been mocked and humiliated by God the Father. In a sort of re-extension of the dream, Confucius was made literally the whipping boy. He was whipped on the orders of God, humiliated publicly. So it was necessary to be against Confucius but in favor of the best sides of the morality that he had instilled. And that is part of the intellectual endeavor that was undertaken by the Taiping.

Knowledge of the West

Another category would be knowledge and understanding of the West, although I think perhaps that knowledge of the West might be less important than most of the others. After 1856, the West in Hong Kong became very important in the Taiping movement. Because Hong Kong flourished under British colonial rule and in fact was made into a booming, international harbor (its take-off period was in the 1850s), several new recruits to the Taiping movement who were related to Hong and also Hakka came from Hong Kong. They brought the news of what British organizational theory and practice were able to do with what in 1840 had been, to use a phrase from the negotiation, a barren and pestilential rock on which nothing would grow. By 1855 it was a boomtown, and there was something to be learned from this. The Taiping began to wonder if they could borrow from that.

Hong was in an area where the West was developing its own community on the edge of Canton City, and he was very much aware of some of their firepower. But his main knowledge of the West—and this is either a separate crosshead or a related one—was his awareness of missionaries and what they were doing. Again, though I'm staying away from the word coincidence, another of our intersections is that the Protestant missionaries began to arrive in large numbers around 1806, just before he was born, in an area near where Hong lived. By the 1820s they were in considerable numbers. These were mainly American and British Protestant missionaries with a scattering of Central European Protestant missionaries and a very few Catholics. But the Catholic great mission days were in fact over by this time, though they were to resume later; this was the Protestant time of ascendancy. A lot of this impetus was Baptist. In fact, one of the most important influences on Hong was a Tennessee Baptist who had taught himself Hakka dialect and was preaching in the area at this time. There were also a large number of Scottish missionaries, who were often Presbyterian. These groups of missionaries were learning Chinese and they were spearheading the teaching of Christianity at the time. And they were translating the Bible with Chinese assistants as they learned the language, and they were beginning to create tracts.

Distribution

Linked to this, but you can call it a separate category I think, would be the aggressive distribution of those tracts. I use the word aggressive mainly in the sense of vigorous, though sometimes it was downright aggressive. There are ways you can be handed that text: you can have it shoved at you; you can have somebody say "Would you like to drop by my place and pick up a tract?" or they can come to you and make sure you get the tract. If you're away, they can either go away or they can shove the tract under the door. The Protestants were doing all the latter. They were pushing the tracts, they were shoving them on village doorsteps, they were—as I found to my great amazement, but almost amusement—emulating little Moses in the bulrushes by putting tracts in tiny rafts and floating them down the rivers so that a Chinese fisherman would pick them up. They were throwing them up in the air above Chinese crowds so that people would just put their hands up for the tracts and, so to speak, Providence would decide who got the tract. Or, and this is where many bits of the story run together, a few very smart Chinese converts at the time said, 'look, if we want to reach the elite of China, the young, bright, educated men, where do we find them?' And they came up with an answer that was correct. They said 'at the local examinations. There is nowhere else you're going to get so many well-educated, potentially influential young people.' But these were people who were well on the way to passing the exams. And in that group was the young Hong from his Hakka village trying to pass the exams—that's why he was at the right place at the right time. If the word "right" is right. We'll decide on that later.

Content of Christianity

Then there's the content of Christianity itself, which surely is a crosshead. What was it that the message was spreading here? I've tried to suggest already that it was an extraordinarily volatile mix; to use a phrase current with social anthropologists, it was an "unmediated mix." There was no attempt to explain the direction or the purpose of what these religious texts were. There was no suggestion of what the organization should be.

So Hong and his followers in the God Worshipping community, and then in the Taiping community, had to construct the organizational mechanisms that were not explained to them in these unmediated texts. But they also identified with them in a very personal way. And lastly, there would be a military awareness, an awareness of a different technology in warfare, a different deadliness to warfare. I have a chapter in my new book trying to intersect military history with the Bible. For instance, I think you can juxtapose Hong's reading of the prophet Isaiah with the reality of military clashes at the time, because that's exactly what Hong was doing. Is it right for us as historians to pursue that? I think it is. Hong was reading the first chapter of Isaiah and at the same time he was witness to this devastating new type of warfare. And we find, in a recently discovered Taiping text, a strange message from on high: Hong discusses with Jesus the fact that "a general from the west" is going to come to help the Taiping. This is an astonishing remark that we'd never had in any other Taiping text, but this is an authenticated text. A general from the West is going to come and help the Taiping. And Hong says to Jesus, "Who is the general? What's his name?" Jesus sensibly says It's not time to tell you yet. You'll know when that moment comes. Well, the moment never did come. But that hope, I think, may be part of the story of why the British were respected, because they were the firepower in the area. Supposing a British general, one of those people blowing the Manchus apart, seizing the city of Canton, seizing Hong Kong, supposing such a man was to come over to the Taiping. What would happen next? So that question is sort of hanging over our story. And it links to a final one, which we will deal with tomorrow. What if, in the middle of all these intersections, you self-identify—with increasing specificity—with the stories and the characters in the Bible itself? For that's what Hong came to do.

* * * * *

Questions and Answers

Question: You spoke of three people in Hong's dream, an older man whose name was God and a younger man whose name was Jesus. Was the older woman Mary?

Spence: No. This gets us into a complex area, but I think we can deal with this now, because we've got lots to talk about tomorrow. The older woman seems to have been God's wife. Now, we're dealing here with an area in which the Chinese family is being transposed to the language of the Bible, and in which the idea of virgin birth is not really discussed by the Taiping. So really what Hong is finding on high and finding in the Bible is a divine family of which he is going to become a part. So the older woman who ritually cleanses him so that he can go and see his father, is what, in Hong's way—and he would have meant this totally unblasphemously or unmockingly—would have been Mrs. God. And God and Mrs. God had a son and the son is Jesus. So we have a complete vaulting over Joseph and Mary and other aspects of the story. Jesus is God's son, and there's a logic to this. Because if God had a wife so that he could have a family, it must be legitimate and straightforward, he must be married. Then there is Jesus, and there's Hong as the brother, the two kids. Hong is married—he was married on earth—what about Jesus? Well, a newly discovered text has one half page in which Hong discusses and asks after Mrs. Jesus. I find it remarkably beautiful and powerful; a strange passage. It helped me a lot to try and understand Hong. Obviously, Jesus also is a powerful force, a God-man. But he also needs a family, he can't just stay up there. Hong knows about the crucifixion, the resurrection; that is all in the Bible for him to read in the New Testament. But only in this text does he give Jesus a wife, and mention that Jesus and Mrs. Jesus have five children. He does not give their names, which would have been absolutely electrifying, but their ages are given, which is interesting enough, and their genders. So we know that Jesus had three boys and two girls. Their ages run from teenagers down to the age of about nine. They are spaced sensibly about two years apart. And Hong in this text says "How are the kids?" And Jesus says "They're fine, thanks. The oldest boy is now fifteen." I mean it's a conversation any of us might have: The oldest boy is fifteen. Oh goodness, how he must have grown. And then the next boy is thirteen and then there's a first girl, she's about eleven. I find this more than absorbing; I find it taking us right to the edge of possible history, and the understanding of another human being. But it takes us to a really amazing mystery that I might share with you here. . . .

When Hong had that dream in 1837, a year after being given the text and apparently not absorbing all of it but at least looking at it, there is absolutely tantalizing evidence that Hong had a wife, a first wife. He was by this time twenty-three and it would be very, very unlikely in rural China not to have married by twenty-three, though if you were poor and still struggling with exams it's ambiguous. But it seems probable that he was married, of course, in a marriage arranged by his family. All of these marriages would have been arranged by the parents. And very shortly afterwards, perhaps just before his dream, his wife died in childbirth, and the child also died. It was a boy child. . . .

In 1848, eleven years later, we have a separate text in which Hong is talking again about heaven, about his heavenly wife. But this was eleven years after the dream; and Hong, in talking about Jesus's family and what is going on in the heavenly realm, is met by a woman who looks at him really grievingly and says, "Don't you recognize me?" and Hong says, "Wait a minute." And she says, "I'm your first wife. I'm your First Chief Moon." He says, "Oh yes, how are things?" And she says, "You don't even ask me about our son." And he says, "Our son. How is our son?" And she says, "Well, he's now eleven." In other words, the heavenly child, if there is such a thing in his belief system, is proven by two texts to be exactly eleven years old, just as he should be if the wife had died in childbirth at the moment of the dream in which he went to heaven. What I find even more moving, though I'll never be able to prove this and I don't dare say it in my book, is that if Jesus and Mrs. Jesus had five children, and they're spaced the way they are, Hong's dead but divine child, now aged eleven, has a family of playmates. In other words, the little boy at eleven is in a family of teenagers whose ages go down to about nine. So he's in a perfect position for a compassionate and cheerful extended family system. That is going far to the edge of history, but it fits with the texts.

It's in that context that we don't have the Virgin Mary, we don't have Joseph, though Hong did know the Bible story, and the Christmas story. We have this complex structuring of a nuclear family with a heavenly dimension and an earthly dimension. And he always called his Taiping wife the Second Chief Moon, and she's later made the empress in their Taiping kingdom. She's treated with respect, though Hong later takes many other consorts as a sort of heavenly emperor on earth, and that upset many of the missionaries and some of his early followers. But this wife was the mother of his legitimate children on earth. So the Second Chief Moon bears him four children, and the boy who is their earthly son is made the young heavenly king. He is, in fact, the second king of the Taiping kingdom on earth until, after his father's death, he is destroyed by the Qing. So your question cuts right into the heart of this, but shows us the complexity of trying to analyze what is going on here.

Question: As you've been speaking, I've been thinking a lot about the recent unfortunate past of Waco, Texas, in regard to a certain new interpreter of the Bible—David Koresh and the Davidians—and I was just wondering if Hong had a vision of the end of time in his, and what that was.

Spence: Since we are here in Waco, one's thoughts do go to David Koresh and what happened to the Branch Davidians. But the question is more specifically what about the end of time. What is Hong's vision of the end of time?

Hong's vision about time and what is going to happen on earth is very much colored by the book of Revelation. Well, you can interpret the text in so many ways, but it has an immense destructive, chaotic center. It is brilliantly conceived, in literary terms, but terrifying in terms of destruction of a huge percentage of those on earth and then the final coming of the saints. Hong, I think, was drawn to that kind of an interpretation. In seeking the promised land on earth, he wouldn't tell his followers where it was, but when they got to Nanjing, he said, "There it is," and Nanjing's name was changed to Tianjing, Heavenly Capital, Heavenly Capital on earth. But he also told his followers that this was a holding station. Nanjing was an earthly paradise, but nobody should muddle that up with life in the true celestial paradise. And in the fullness of time, God would call the Taiping followers from their heavenly earthly paradise, their Tianjing on the Yangzi River, up to his kingdom.

Hong also had a series of remarks which he took from the tract by the Chinese convert, and I've often thought one could do a whole study just on this. It's very difficult, but it's germane to your question. . . . Near the end of the extraordinary tract in nine little fascicles that was given to Hong, the author says that what's going to happen to our country of China is that it's just going to be fragmented. It's going to be broken up like chaff in the wind because people are ungodly and unfaithful. And then the author says "Look what happened to the kingdom of Israel. Look what happened to God's children because they did not keep his word and they strayed." And he says just as the kingdom of Israel was fragmented and the Jews have had to wander all over the world, so China is going to be torn apart by these forces and the Chinese are going to become the wanderers. He says the only way we can prevent that is by tending to God's true religion, putting our house in order, putting our families in order and our countrymen, and thus averting this catastrophe to our nation. But at the same time he says that the foreigners—and you wouldn't have thought this was possible really in a Chinese text at the time, but it's there—the foreigners or the people from the West have been bringing a good religion, so we must separate that from the warfare and the hostility to China. That may be where Hong's refusal to think so negatively of the British came from—because the author of the tract, Liang, had been converted by a British missionary and saw in this very rigorous sort of British Protestantism a hope for life in Asia. Hong's only contact with a missionary in person, until near the end of his life, was with a Southern Baptist, Isachar Roberts, who was a Tennessee fundamentalist Baptist. Roberts did give Hong some Bible classes. Alas, we don't know exactly what happened. . . .

Roberts began preparing Hong for baptism, and in preparing for baptism the minister should, and very often does prepare a kind of spiritual chart, a spiritual progress chart with the potential for baptism; they can work on it together or the converts, in this case, can develop it themselves. Hong apparently did this, and Roberts had it in his house, and his house was broken into in the trouble (there was a new burst of fighting in the late 1840s), and all his papers were burned. But we might have had, of all incredible documents, Hong's personal testimony as transcribed by and shared with the Tennessee Baptist from the 1840s. It would have been one of the most extraordinary documents for a historian to ponder, but it's gone.

For reasons we don't understand, Roberts refused to baptize Hong. Something happened; there are many stories about what happened and I won't go into them now, but one of them seems to involve Hong being a bit greedy for money from the Christians. But that depends on how you feel about Hong. It doesn't fit with the other side we know of him at this stage of his life, but it might be true. Whatever happened, Roberts, having prepared him for baptism, withdrew, saying he was not yet ready. Hong then went off and it was in that time that he began to draw closer to his own followers and say, well, we can baptize each other, if those ministers won't do it. We know what to do. They got the general idea. Roberts had planned total immersion, of course, in the waters off Canton harbor in the Pearl River. And in Roberts's letters, we've recently found one about the joy of taking the Chinese down to the delta area as the moon rises and baptizing them, and the rolling surf, and so on. It's a very powerful passage. And that's what Hong was denied. So he chose a local mountain stream with two friends. But they felt that was enough for God—they felt this would be acceptable. I think we can truly say that. They didn't come back to the regular church.

Once they seized Nanjing Hong invited Roberts to join them. We've got our kingdom on earth, please come and join us. And Roberts spent the next nine years of his life trying to get there. The whole place was surrounded, there was warfare everywhere. Roberts was married and had a child himself, and his family didn't think this was a great idea. But he tried to get through the different opposing armies, he tried to get up to Shanghai, tried to cut down the Yangzi, but he was prevented by the Americans who had neutrality agreements with the Qing dynasty about shipping. The British thought he was not to be trusted, and then finally, in about 1862, near the fall of the kingdom, Roberts got through and met Hong again. Alas, we don't know exactly what was said, but Roberts apparently felt humiliated by whatever Hong said to him. And from his feeling uncharitable, one might say Hong gave as good as he got twelve years earlier. But we don't know what happened. Roberts left in great humiliation and real fury in 1863. It's a very strange story. Roberts must have given him a vision as well of this everlasting kingdom.

Question: You talked about the vision that he kept having, those psychic visions. And I was curious: was he sick when he got this or did he keep having them all the time? Did he go into a state? What exactly were they?

Spence: The question was about these visions, was he sick when he had them, did he go on having them all the time, right? And did they stop or come and go? Part of the trouble is we can only go on what is recorded about the visions, either by Hong himself (which was quite a lot) or by his followers, who wrote the kind of texts about him that one would expect in such a religious environment, or some later pronouncements that he issued, and bits and pieces of gossip about what was going on in the heavenly kingdom. Obviously, whether he was sick at the time of the first vision takes us right to the heart of psychological intersections with spiritual experiences or alleged spiritual experiences. And again, with sickness we have to decide what we mean, what we now call mental illness, or some kind of physiological imbalance. I nowhere in the book use a word like insane, as I didn't in *The Question of Hu*,[2] except when people accused him of being insane. But I don't judge this. This book is an attempt to see if one can find the logic of Hong's belief pattern and his actions, extraordinary actions. Maybe one can't, in which case the whole thing would better not to have been attempted. But I feel you can, particularly because of the new texts we've found.

Let's say in 1837 he had this long series of dreams, of visions. We know this from his family via a text that then assumed sacred weight. We are still faced with the same sort of problem we have in deciding exactly where in Bethlehem the stall was, where exactly Joseph was. We have here a divine story, but one full of existential details, homey details, practical details we'll never be able to prove or disprove. The mythic takes over from the story. But according to Hong's family—his brothers and also his mother, whose words were then incorporated in a Taiping text—when he came back from that exam in 1837 I think we can safely say he was prostrate with depression. He was just gone, he was flat out. He couldn't copy anymore. Each of these phrases is a loaded one, tugging us in a different direction. He'd had a breakdown. I'm not sure which of these words is right. He did take to his bed. He said he was exhausted. He lay down and, according to some people, he lay as if dead. And his family feared for his life. Then when he tracks back into the story, he went on this journey, thinking he was dying. It looks as if he was sliding in and out of a coma. He made some remarks to his family which include a remark to a wife, saying "My wife, you're expecting a child. If I don't come back, my brothers, elder brothers, will help you look after it." That would be a normal remark in most family situations if you felt the end was near, except that the only marriage we know about came later and the children are all much older than nine months at the most from the dream. So it may be somehow related to the death or the illness of the wife in childbirth. "Our child is dying, I am dying." We don't know. But that would have led to an increase in depression.

If he seemed comatose—and again, I'm using the word as a very general term—but if he was comatose, then he may have roused himself by the action of striking down the demons, because his family agree, if the text is accurate, that he actually leapt from his bed and slashed around waving his hands and shouting. And then after a long time, as it might be after an intense fever or depression or breakdown, he apparently came to. Not exactly "Where was I" because he knew where he was; he looked around and said "Oh, you're all still here." And his family watched out for him. The family had to watch him. I could have added this to the context lecture, because if we take a context of the legal history in the Qing dynasty the family were totally responsible for the behavior of what we might call an unbalanced member of the family, or an insane member. The state did not think it was its business to look after the mentally unwell. It was the family's responsibility. But if the mentally unwell caused any damage or killed people or stole or caused property damage, the family was responsible. It was a very double-edged responsibility. The result of this was that in some cases you got what the West considered outrageous treatment of the mentally unbalanced in China. They would be locked in their rooms or in some cases literally bricked into a space, so they could be fed and cleaned occasionally. Because if that person got out and killed a villager, all the family could be executed by the Qing law of responsibility, a family responsibility. So the family, we can believe, would have kept a very close eye on him and they continued to keep a close eye on him when he came out of it, whatever it was he came out of.

But he remembered the dreams. There was never again, to answer the second part of the question, there was never again a dream of that absolute intensity, at least he never told us about it. Once he'd absorbed this, these dreams were rewritten and shifted around, but probably in his dream he wrote down his new name, a name that this older man in heaven gave him and in that new name this figure that he later identified with God the Father told him to change his middle name. Now what is genuinely, I shouldn't say spooky, but mysterious, is that the name that Hong's parents gave him as a little boy was Hong Huo Xiu. But when he read the Bible, he found Huo is the middle name of Jehovah, Yeh-huo-hua. So Hong learned, and I can only imagine his appalled horror, that he had God's name, and that's not something to be lightly borne. Right? So he changed it, or felt it should be changed. And from then on he's never again called Hong Huo anything. He's called Hong Xiuquan. So his last name becomes his middle name and he adds the Quan, which is what the person who turned out to be God told him to do. "Quan" means complete or absolute or total, and is the central word, I think it's in Psalm 19, which then became Hong's favorite psalm. So part of the self-identification with the Bible is what we might call a kind of name magic in which you have to escape the name of God which in all innocence you've borne, but in all honesty you must get rid of.

Hong had many other trips, they're more like short trips, to heaven. And for most of the rest of his life the dreams were brought down by his two closest lieutenants, the two closest aides in his heavenly kingdom. One of these men claimed to relay the words of Jesus, and the other to relay the words of God through the Holy Spirit or the Holy Ghost. So the later texts we have are usually words from on high, coming down to Hong through these two other men. And that is much closer to what we call a shamanic vision. But Hong still occasionally had dreams, and then near the end of his life his son began to have them too. Whether this was auto-suggestion or what, I don't know. But Hong began to publicize his son's dreams—that's the earthly son—because of course he wanted his son to succeed as the new earthly king. So a new series of visions appeared very near the end of Hong's life. And it's very hard to gauge them. Also, his earthly wife had dreams, which Hong then began to announce to his people. So the historian, being a bit cynical, might say that as Hong was really losing his power and felt that his kingdom was being destroyed, which began to happen around 1861, he suddenly felt the need to have an awful lot more visions, to reassert this connection with heaven. These new visions came after he'd killed on of the intermediaries and the other one had been killed in combat. So he's now got to struggle himself to reach God on high.

One Taiping historian has used a very beautiful sentence: "The trouble with Hong is that once these intermediaries die, God fell silent."[3] And what could be more terrifying for somebody who has been in regular contact, to have that God falling silent as you're waiting. Suddenly the messages stop. And that stillness must have been terrifying, I think. That is the sort of negative religious experience that perhaps he went through, and he counteracted it by new dreams, or really the depression led him to have a new burst of dreams. We'll never know.

Notes to Lecture I

1. Tracking the Heavenly City; see Jonathan Spence, *God's Chinese Son: The Taiping Heavenly Kingdom of Hong Xiuquan* (New York, 1996), chapter 6.

2. Jonathan Spence, *The Question of Hu* (New York, 1988).

3. The dreams and intermediaries are discussed by Rudolf G. Wagner in *Reenacting the Heavenly Vision: The Role of Religion in the Taiping Rebellion* (Berkeley, 1982).

LECTURE II

RULING THE EARTHLY PARADISE

I want to start by spending a few moments, for those not here yesterday, to say we're talking about a rebellion, a revolutionary movement in the nineteenth century called the Taiping, which reached its height between 1853 and 1864. It was ruled by a self-styled heavenly king who had learned through his encounter with Christian religious texts that he was not only a religious leader, but he was the younger brother of Jesus, and that this had given him a special power. Thus, he was literally God's Chinese Son, which is the name I chose for my book. Yesterday we looked at all the contexts that had to flow together to make it possible for him to rise with an army in the south of China, advance up to the Yangzi River, and march and take boats down the river and along its banks until he seized one of China's largest cities, Nanjing. He made it his heavenly capital on earth for an astonishing eleven years, until the whole enterprise collapsed in fire and sword with a kind of apocalyptic vision that one might have expected, and which perhaps he welcomed. That is the background. So having done the contexts yesterday in what I hope was some of its richness, I would like today to see how Hong came to rule this earthly paradise and what steps along the way led to this growth. The sub-heading for this study might be called "the logic of growth" or "trying to chart the logic." I should say that there are some who would say that Hong Xiuquan, the leader of this uprising, essentially cannot be studied; that his life pushes us over the edge of what is the knowable and the understandable. But I tend to like challenges like that, and when I encounter something very hard to understand, I like, if possible, not to dismiss it and not to give it a label like insane or incomprehensible, but to try and see if there is any way of charting the growth of a personality behind such events.

One other detail is that Hong was born in 1814. We do know a lot about this religious leader as a man, as a human, as a family man, his background, and it is thus possible to have a kind of biographical underpinning even for a story as strange as this. So let us try and explore what I think can be recreated as a kind of intellectual odyssey, even if it is of a kind that is most unusual. It led to enormous hopes, but also enormous destruction, as this heavenly kingdom was founded on earth in the China of the nineteenth century. And I'm going to try and take us through a sequence that is pretty much chronological, because, as I mentioned yesterday, I still believe in dates in history, I still believe in organizing across time chronologically and then cutting through it in as many ways as you want to. We're trying to get a sense of individual movement across time, whether it's of individual lives or institutions or a broad social movement.

So we have here what I hope is a kind of intellectual odyssey of this young man called Hong from the years of his childhood. As I tried to show yesterday, his life intersected with aspects of Christian belief and Bible reading, and he attempted to draw all these elements together until he had founded the kingdom, and then in a sense presided over its ruin.

The point we must begin with here sounds very simple, but it's actually one of the great conundrums and difficulties of Chinese history. My brief note says "basic literacy for Hong leading to reading skills." I think in our culture we'd have a pretty good sense of what that meant, basic literacy leading to more advanced reading skills. In China, that's something much harder to be clear about. Where does literacy lead to something like real reading skills? What is literacy? Dealing with a language of written characters, a calligraphic structure of language, nonalphabetic, what is the minimal vocabulary for such a phrase as basic literacy? The argument is hot and heavy on this topic right now in our field. And it's a fascinating topic, because it forces us to decide what elements of vocabulary we need to have in a given culture to be full members of it. It's not just as simple as knowing your arithmetic, or some basic reading and writing. In China, you've got to marshal increasing numbers of written characters that get you higher and higher in the scale of readership. To give you two examples of the scale: it is said by many that with eight hundred to a thousand characters, one can handle various kinds of rather simple texts. But those have to be written in the context of the vocabulary that only needs about that many characters. As soon as you get into any specialized sub-field—for instance, real estate or politics, commercial ventures, aesthetics, philosophy—you have to add a completely new set of vocabularies. It's the same for the mathematics, the sciences, and so on. All of them will have different aspects. At the highest level, when you're trying to read all the texts of the past and make sense of the whole classical Chinese tradition, as many Western scholars pointed out to their horror and other Chinese reinforced with a cheerful smile, it helps to have about thirty thousand characters. With twenty thousand you can do pretty well, and with ten thousand and a battery of dictionaries you might be able to cope. But this is daunting, and it gives enormous advantage to those from elite backgrounds, who can have an advanced technical education with very fine teaching. So the dominance of education as a value in the Chinese culture is linked to the complexity of attaining an advanced level of ability to read difficult texts.

Hong was somebody whose basic literacy was hard bought, since he was from a farming family. But he was able to push his way through the limitations of his background in essentially a village school situation, and get to the level where he could pass the qualifying exams. One of the premises of my book is that whereas many scholars have talked about Hong as a failed scholar, I see him as a triumphant village school boy. I think that is a huge difference in how we want to look at it. Yes, "failed scholar" if you're a member of the elite and your friends are going to the advanced levels, getting their doctorates. But if you've grown up in an area where almost nobody can read and write at all, how amazing to pass the qualifying exam. And yet, how sad also not to be able to rise higher. So basic literacy is an essential part of this story. Hong had the reading skills that would enable him to tackle some of the basic classics of the time, to have a good memorized knowledge of Confucian texts, to be able to browse, if he chose, through Buddhist texts or the texts of the Daoist tradition. This also made it possible that when a missionary pushed a tract into his hand—it was a summary of Christian belief in Chinese—Hong was able to read it. It's absolutely essential that those two things flow together to make any sense of this story.

The vocabulary was large in that Christian tract. It was not limited to a thousand basic characters. As I mentioned yesterday, it introduced a bewildering number of names—religious names, biblical names—that Hong had to try and spell out and think through for himself.

Building on this basic literacy, then, and the mental skill that would lead him to be able to read his way into Christian texts, we can analyze his local religious background in local practice and local theory. Hong would have been raised in an area in southeast China with a bewildering mass of religions. I mentioned just now Daoist and Buddhist elements. There would also have been those elements of Confucian ceremonial that were not just philosophical, but partook of the ritual elements that have led some people to say Confucianism has aspects of a religion to it. That debate is also hot and heavy and complicated. But he would have known about the ritualistic side of Confucius. He would have known about all the disciples of Confucius whose tablets were arranged in great rows around the Confucian temple in his native town where he studied. And he would have known the whole roster of religious festivals based on the Chinese calendar, the lunar calendar, that would have surrounded him from his infancy. These introduced a maze of gods and goddesses and spirits, or relationships between the humans and the cosmos, the need to bring rain, to bring sun, to bring crops, all in a kind of cosmic rhythm that was linked to your own mediating power, that of your lineage, that of your clergy, that of the representatives of the state. So his religious upbringing, in a very broad sense, would have been rich and complex.

Then there is another element; I would call it straightforwardly his vision of hell. When Hong was young, this vision of hell was represented in popularized folk Buddhist texts called the Yuli texts, the *Jade Record* texts. Just as the secret societies I mentioned last time were spreading in China, so were these underground *Jade Record* texts circulating, spreading an extraordinary tale of an end that was not quite endless, but a long drawn-out torment of trial and testing that must come to all of us when we die and go to the underworld—good and bad alike. We will have to explain all our actions before nine interlocking underworld courts, presided over by terrifying judges with their staffs, who will each investigate different aspects of our actions on earth, looking for the violations that we've committed. All kinds of patterns of our behavioral relation to society, to the land, the sky, belief practice, trade, commerce, law, all of our sexual behavior—all of them would be examined. All of us would be punished. Hong would have expected as a child to be punished for these various violations. And then, at the end of this huge cycle of trial and punishment, we would be reborn on earth to make our way all over again. So this became a transmigration of souls religion in these texts, at the very end of this horrendous depiction of the suffering that we all have to endure. The compassionate side of that was that just before returning to earth after our travails, we would go to the temple of forgetting. In the temple of forgetting the goddess Meng would purge us of the knowledge of the suffering we'd undergone, and also of all the experiences in our previous life that brought that suffering. So when we were reborn it would be as we all are, ignorant of our previous existences, though we would perhaps guess from the travails in our present life what we might have done to deserve the pains that we are enduring.

This was an extraordinarily complicated pattern of religious belief. We know that Hong knew these Yuli texts, because he makes a remark expressly singling them out for destruction once he becomes heavenly king. Since I'm an historian who loves working backwards, when I saw Hong order these texts to be destroyed, I determined to find out what they were. And the quest led me to this fascinating body of material, this *Jade Record* background of text and religious experience.

On top of that, there would be Daoist imagery, because Daoism was not just a nonmundane, or natural equivalence, religion. It had its own highly complex imagery, its own pantheons of gods, its own extraordinary metaphors and allegories for the human experience. And these Daoist elements were also combined in Hong's mind with the literacy, with the local festival and other practices. Because in the dream he had in 1837 when he had certain visions, he was drawn by all these different interlocking memories into a visionary journey into another world where he encountered various figures who, six years later, he learned to identify with God the Father and Jesus, and he made the decision from textual and other evidence that satisfied his whole mind that he was Jesus's younger brother. That structuring of a relationship that many of us might find shocking or incomprehensible, grew to him out of the intersection of Christian texts with Daoist and other imagery and these elements of personal belief.

Round about 1843, when Hong was in his late twenties, he read with care the Christian tracts that he'd been given. These Christian tracts—again I have to repeat a fragment from yesterday—were a summary written in Chinese of aspects of the Bible; often whole chapters were literally translated into Chinese, with a commentary by a Chinese Christian convert, not explaining the text, but talking about different elements of the Bible story. It was this text that Hong was given and that he kept. As I mentioned yesterday, he didn't throw it away—he kept this text. So when he was ready, we might say, he read it. In fact a friend urged him to read it. He read it, and he found that the Bible text in Chinese made sense to him of his dreams and of his various yearnings. But I also think it must have been extraordinarily baffling. And I want to try and suggest the way that I as an historian tried to create this sense of bewilderment by taking two very well-known stories, but putting them in the way that Hong confronted them. Hong was given a little bit of the book of Genesis, selections that included the story of Noah but did not tell him that the ark came to rest. We've got to now think of the Bible as story-telling and then imagine being given a truncated version. Hong was later to read all the Bible in Chinese, but in this period of his young manhood, he was reading these selections. So he was reading this text, after failing his exams again and again, but struggling with all these levels of religious knowledge. And he was presented with a story of Noah's Ark that stops in the middle. Again, remember this about narrative: if we don't know the end of a story, we don't know that it's not ended, do we? We don't know when it's come to a close. At the same time, he was given the story of Lot and his wife and the flight from Sodom and Gomorrah. And I tried to see this through in the context of Hong looking at this passage of Genesis and not being told what happened, but also deciding not to throw the book away and to think it through.

One other thing that has to be explained here is that when Hong read this first part of the Bible, he encountered a name for God that would have been very hard for him to make any sense of. The Chinese characters are *Yeh-huo-hua*, which were used by the Protestant missionaries to render Jehovah in Chinese characters. And the *huo*, the second name for God, was in fact Hong's given name. So he changed his name when he realized that he unwittingly had shared the name of God. He declared his guilt in a way, though it was not his fault. But he immediately took care to change the name. And this *huo* means fire. It's unambiguous; many characters have many meanings in China, but *huo* simply means fire; he had been called young man of fiery talent by his parents. The text gave God's name as being *huo*, the fire, as if Jehovah were full of fire. It would have been very hard to make sense of this, but he would have seen this element. And Hong's own name, the name that he kept all his life, *hong*, also means flood or great flood, and *hong* is the word used for the flood that God sends to punish the people on earth when Noah builds the ark. So Hong is confronted by a flood that is his name in the context of a God whose name he unwittingly shares. When he's confronted with the text, these levels must draw together. Let me just quote you a little bit; this passage we know was in the text that he read:

How enraged this god has been, Liang's book tells Hong, enraged at the sins of those he has created. Only one man, named Noah, found favor in this god's eyes, for Noah alone of all those on earth followed the true path or righteousness. Noah was already six hundred years old when this god told him to build a boat, and though so old, he obeyed at once. His three sons helped him. The boat was huge, three stories high, three hundred feet long and fifty broad. There was a window in the boat, and a great door, and all the animals came in, seven by seven or two by two, and all the birds, and pairs of all the creeping things. And Noah joined them, with his wife, and his three sons, and his three sons' wives. The god's flood covered the whole earth. Except for those inside the boat, the god killed everyone. The god's flood killed the giants, who lived on the earth in those days, killed all the other animals and birds and creeping things. Only in their boat, above the mountaintops, eight people floated free, just eight in one family, they and the creatures they brought with them.

Hong's second name is there in other places too, for another god—described as "the highest Lord of all"—sent fire to destroy two cities with curious names, just as Yeh-huo-hua had sent the flood to destroy the people of the earth. Like the first, this god was angry, for the people of these two cities gave themselves to lust and wildness, leaving no depravity unexplored; with his fire the god destroyed them, every trace, every person, every house, and finally the very soil itself, converting the land into a monstrous lake. But once again the god chose one family to be saved, that of a man named Lot. Lot had a wife, and two daughters, and god saved all four; till Lot's wife looked back at the blazing cities and was turned to salt. So only three remained.

> Liang's book does not say what happened at the end of either story. What of that family of eight? What of the animals and birds crowded in around them? Did they float thus through all eternity? Did they ride the waves in their enormous boat, beneath the rain-sodden sky, forever and a day, skin and fur and feathers, until they became one with the water, the wood, and the wind?
>
> And why salt?
>
> Hong fails the examinations. He keeps the book.[1]

To me that is one of the mysteries of our story, that this information is flowing in; and it must have been, I feel, something like that creation of the text as summarized through his eyes. The key point is that he keeps the book, he doesn't say "This is incomprehensible." He keeps it and it becomes the basis for his life.

So in this intersection of text and literacy, Hong was able to read that story and think it through, and wait for the key to come. And the key came later, two or three years later, when he got a copy of the entire Bible in Chinese, again prepared by missionaries in the Canton area. Protestant missionaries, both British and American, worked together from the King James version to give a running Chinese translation. These missionaries translated all the Bible because it was the Word of God as they understood it, and nothing was to be left out, however difficult. So the translation is a sea of names; it finishes the story of Noah; it finishes the story of Lot in all its detail; and Hong had received this text as he was founding his God Worshippers Society. And by mentioning the God Worshippers Society, we're drawn to the next stage in his life. When he was thirty years old, a small group of believers, touched by Hong's ability to interpret and talk about these texts, gathered around him; only two at first, two believers, rising across a space of about eight years to thirty or forty thousand. These God Worshippers began to read the Bible and think about it, and they also elevated Hong to the role of leader that he had sought. And in this period he had a brief time of formal Bible instruction from a Baptist missionary, a Southern Baptist from Tennessee, who actually gave Hong Bible-reading classes and prepared him for baptism. But the relationship stalled; it came to an end. The Protestant missionary, called Roberts, did not finally give baptism to Hong, so Hong withdrew from his own encounter with an organized church, or at least a qualified pastor. And from then on he reinterpreted for himself. He baptized himself with his friends, and from then on the true believers baptized each of the new believers. They never again brought in a pastor from the outside. There were none available, indeed, because they'd moved deep into the countryside. They now had to be on their own with their divine mission and with God's help.

As that was progressing, Hong was making a number of "jumps" into the text or interpretations of the text. One I mentioned very briefly was the realization and the elaboration of the idea that he was Jesus's younger brother. And this put him in a family relationship with the structure of the Holy Family in the New Testament particularly. But he did not move into also identifying with Mary and Joseph. Instead he treated Jesus as the Son of God, himself as Jesus's younger brother, and both of them as the sons of God on High. So the Holy Family was given a different interpretation. Jesus was given a family, and God was given a family, because Hong remained, in the traditional Chinese way, family-centered and family-oriented. So he pieced together a series of interconnections between himself and the world that he saw as identified and discussed in the Bible. We have now the beginning of a series of what we can call identifications with figures in the Bible as text and as divine word. Jesus is a very early one. Identification of self with Jesus's younger brother. And then, as Hong led his troops northward from their very desperate situation in southeast China, as they moved north up to the Yangzi River, it was inevitable, I think, in Hong's mind, that he would start to identify with a figure in the second book of the Bible, which by now he had read with great care, that is Exodus. And thus, he identified with Moses leading the children from Egypt, the Children of Israel, towards the promised land.

Notes to Lecture II

1. Jonathan Spence, *God's Chinese Son*, pp. 32-33.
2. Spence, pp. 295-296.

JONATHAN D. SPENCE

Professor Jonathan D. Spence was born in England on August 11, 1936. He attended Winchester College in 1949-1954, and after two years in the British Army, studied at Clare College, Cambridge University, receiving his B.A. in History in 1959. At Cambridge, he was editor of the newspaper, *Varsity*, and coeditor of the literary magazine, *Granta*.

Professor Spence received his M.A. and Ph.D. from Yale in 1961 and 1965, respectively, and joined the Yale faculty in 1965. He became the George Burton Adams Professor of History in 1976, the Sterling Professor of History in 1993, and served as chairman of the department from 1983-1986.

Professor Spence's dissertation at Yale won the John Adison Porter Prize and was published by the Yale University Press under the title *Ts'ao Yin and the K'ang-hsi Emperor: Bondservant and Master.* Subsequent publications include *To Change China: Western Advisers in China from 1620-1960* (1969); *Emperor of China: Self Portrait of K'ang-hsi* (1978); *The Gate of Heavenly Peace* (1981); *The Memory Place of Matteo Ricci* (1984); *The Question of Hu* (1988); *The Search for Modern China* (1990); and *God's Chinese Son* (1996).

Professor Spence was Cochairman of the first Yale faculty group that traveled to China in May 1974 and subsequently lectured with two Yale alumni travel groups on tours of China. In the Spring of 1987, he was Visiting Professor at the University of Peking.

He is the recipient of numerous honors and awards, including the William C. DeVane Medal of the Yale Chapter of Phi Beta Kappa (1978), a Guggenheim Fellowship (1979), the Los Angeles Times History Prize (1982), the Vursel Prize of the American Academy and Institute of Arts and Letters (1983), a MacArthur Fellowship (1988), and membership in the Council of Scholars at the Library of Congress (1988).

Previous
CHARLES EDMONDSON HISTORICAL LECTURERS

Paul K. Conkin, University of Wisconsin, 1977–1978: "American Christianity in Crisis: Religious Rationalism and Darwinism"

*Walter LaFeber, Cornell University, 1979–1980: "The Third Cold War: Kissinger Years and Carter Years"

*Martin E. Marty, University of Chicago, 1980–1981: "Religious Crises in Modern America: Modernism and Fundamentalism"

**William H. McNeill, University of Chicago, 1981–1982: "The Great Frontier: Freedom and Hierarchy in Modern Times"

Robert L. Heilbroner, The New School for Social Research, 1982–1983: "Capitalism in Transition: The Twentieth Century"

C. Vann Woodward, Yale University, emeritus, 1983–1984: "Continuing Themes in Southern History: The Strange Career of Jim Crow, 1954–1984; The Burden of Southern History, 1952–1984"

*William E. Leuchtenburg, University of North Carolina, Chapel Hill, 1984–1985: "The 1984 Presidential Election in Historical Perspective: From Civil War to the New Deal; From Franklin Roosevelt to Ronald Reagan"

Peter Gay, Yale University, 1985–1986: "Aggression: Toward a Theory of Aggression; Humor: Aggression at Work"

*Gordon S. Wood, Brown University, 1986–1987: "The Making of the Constitution"

Gerda Lerner, University of Wisconsin, Madison, 1987–1988: "Sex and Class: A Revisionist Perspective"

*Robert Darnton, Princeton University, 1988-1989: "What was Revolutionary about the French Revolution?"

*Stephen B. Oates, University of Massachusetts, Amherst, 1989-1990: "Biography as History"

*Dan T. Carter, Emory University, 1990-1991: "George Wallace, Richard Nixon, and the Transformation of American Politics"

*Geoffrey Alan Hosking, University of London, 1991-1992: "Empire and Nation in Russian History"

*Nell Irvin Painter, Princeton University, 1992-1993: "Soul Murder and Slavery"

*Philip D. Curtin, Johns Hopkins University, 1993-1994: "Why People Move: Migration in African History"

*Franklin W. Knight, Johns Hopkins University, 1994-1995: "Race, Ethnicity, and Class: Forging the Plural Society in Latin America and the Caribbean"

*Printed copies are available from the Baylor University Press.
**Printed copies are available from the Princeton University Press.